The Big
Big Cats
Book for Kids

BELLANOVA

MELBOURNE · SOFIA · BERLIN

www.bellanovabooks.com

Big Cats: The Big Book of Big Cats

101+ Amazing Facts about Lions, Tigers, Leopards, Jaguars and Snow Leopards

ISBN: 978-619-264-063-7

Imprint: Bellanova Books

Copyright © 2026 by Jenny Kellett

All rights reserved. No part of this book may be reproduced in any form by any electronic or mechanical means including photocopying, recording, or information storage and retrieval without permission in writing from the author.

Thank you to the following photographers for the beautiful images in this book:

Benh Lieu Song
Clément Bardot
Kevin Pluck
Luca Galuzzi
Sadman Amin
Sharp Photography:
sharpphotography.co.uk
S. Taheri
David Vraju
Hans Stieglitz
HKandy
J. Patrick Fischer
Ltshears
Cburnett
Katie Chan
Lee Elvin
Pascal Blachier
Arturo de Frias Marques
Axel Tschentscher
Rute Martins
Helena Lopes
Pascal Mauerhofer
Tambako

CONTENTS

Introduction	6
Lions	8
Tigers	28
Jaguars	46
Leopards	60
Snow Leopards	76
Spot the difference!	88
Word search	90
Solutions	92
Spot the Difference	92
Thank you!	93
Also by Jenny Kellett	94
Sources	95

INTRODUCTION

Big cats, little cats, fluffy cats and hairless cats, they're all adorable. But we know what you're here for—the big ones!

Big cats are a group of five cats that belong to the Panthera genus (a group of similar animals). These cats are lions, tigers, jaguars, leopards, and snow leopards. Some people also include other large cats like cougars, clouded leopards, and cheetahs in this group, however, that is not correct.

Despite being in the same family, the five big cats are different in many ways, including weight, habitat and appearance.

So, let's find out more about these amazing cats! Are you ready? Let's go!

LIONS

Lions are the mightiest of the big cats, and are often called the 'king of beasts' with good reason! The lion features heavily in ancient mythology and popular culture as a symbol of courage and strength.

Animal Profile

Scientific name: *panthera leo*

Lifespan: 10-15 years in the wild; 20 years in captivity

Conservation status: Vulnerable

Location: African lions: Sub-Saharan Africa. A small population of Asiatic lions live in and around Gir National Park, western India.

A lioness.

The average male lion weighs between 160-225 kg (350-496 lb), depending on where they are from. Southern African lions are the heaviest.

•••

The average female lion weighs between 110-143 kg (240-316 lb).

•••

The heaviest lion ever recorded weighed an incredible 375kg (827 lb).

•••

Lions are the second fastest land mammals in Africa — they can reach speeds of up to 81 km/h (50.3 mph), but only in very short bursts.

•••

The roar of a lion can be heard 8 km (5 miles) away.

Lions roar mostly at night time and they do it to let others know they are there.

•••

Lions don't only roar. They make a range of noises, including purring, bleating, humming and puffing.

•••

Most wild lions can be found in southern and eastern Africa, however, their numbers are rapidly decreasing. In the late half of the 20th century, lion numbers decreased by an estimated 30-50%.

•••

Researchers estimate there are 16,500 and 47,000 lions living in the wild in Africa today.

Unlike other cat species, lions are very sociable. They usually live in prides that include males, females and a few cubs. Lions spend an average of two hours a day walking and 50 minutes eating.

•••

Like the domestic cat, lions spend a lot of time resting — up to 20 hours a day!

An African lioness with its cub.

Lions are most active just after dusk. This is when they usually do their hunting.

•••

Male lions have distinctive manes, while female lions do not.

•••

There might not be any lions living in the wild in Europe, but many European countries have a lion as their national animal, including Bulgaria, Albania, England, Luxembourg, Belgium and the Netherlands.

•••

Evidence from cave paintings suggests that lions didn't always have a mane. In fact, the mane may have evolved 320,000–190,000 years ago.

Different species within the panthera genus (which includes the other big cats) have been cross-bred to produce new breeds such as ligers, tigons, leopons and jaglions. Males from hybrid breeds are usually infertile.

•••

White lions exist, but they are very rare. They have a genetic condition called leucism, which is different to albinism.

•••

Lionesses are better hunters than lions, as they can run 30% faster.

•••

Male lions protect the pride while the lionesses are out hunting.

A lion cub on a tree branch.

A male African lion.

As lions can only run short distances quickly, they get as close as possible to their prey before attacking.

•••

Young lions don't start hunting until they are one year old, and it's not until they are two years old that they are good hunters.

•••

Fossil records show that lions used to exist in Europe and even in Siberia, however they became extinct due to global warming around 11,900 years ago.

•••

Despite being called 'the king of the jungle', there are no lions living in jungles.

•••

The darker a lion's mane, the older it is. A thick, dark mane is a good indication of a healthy lion.

Asiatic lions generally have sparser manes than their African relatives.

•••

Most male West African lions in Pendjari National Park are either maneless or have very short manes.

•••

The word 'Simba' means lion in Swahili. The word also means 'aggressive', 'king' and 'strong.

•••

Lions' heels don't touch the ground when they walk.

•••

The word for lion in Turkish and Mongolian is 'Aslan'. This is also the name of the lion in C.S. Lewis's book The Chronicles of Narnia.

A male lion in Namibia, Africa.

A male lion.

Although they don't love water, lions are great swimmers when they need to cross water.

•••

Wild lions eat between 4.5-11.3 kg (10-25 lbs) of meat a day.

•••

Lions are the only cats that have a tassel on the end of their tails.

•••

Sadly, only one in ten male lions make it to adulthood. The majority die after leaving their pride at the age of two. They are usually kicked out by the older males. Lionesses generally stay behind in the pride.

Lions have great night vision. They can see six times better in the dark than humans! Can you see the white patch under their eyes? This is used to reflect light into their eyes. They also have a reflective coating on the back of their eyes to capture maximum moonlight.

•••

Lions see mostly in blues and greens.

•••

The largest population of lions in Africa is in Tanzania.

•••

Lionesses are pregnant with cubs for around 3.5 months. The typical number of cubs a lioness will have is 3, but it ranges from 1-6.

A young female lion in Serengeti National Park.

Lions come in all different colours, including red, yellow, tan and brown.

•••

A pride has an average of 13 members, but they can range from 2-40 lions.

•••

There are two species of lions still around today — African and Asian.

•••

Lions can't properly roar until the age of two.

A young lion cub.

Home Sweet Home

Lions are known as the 'kings of the jungle', but they actually rule over the savannah. These grassy plains are the perfect hunting grounds. Unlike the dense jungle, the savannah's open landscape allows lions to sneak up on their prey using the tall grasses as cover.

A lion's tawny coat blends into the savannah's golden hues, making it an expert at ambush!

TIGERS

The tiger is the largest cat species in the world. Famous for its beautiful orange and black striped fur, tigers have been an important part of many Asian cultures for centuries. The tiger is one of the 12 Chinese zodiac signs, and plays a key role in many Korean, Buddhist and Hindu rituals and mythology. So what else makes the tiger so fascinating? **Let's find out!**

Animal Profile

Scientific name: Panthera tigris

Lifespan: 10-15 years in the wild; up to 22 years in captivity

Conservation status: Endangered

Location: Across Asia, including Sumatra, India, Nepal, China, Siberia and Myanmar.

Tigers are the largest cat species in the world. They are also the third-largest carnivore on land, behind polar bears and brown bears.

•••

There are 9 subspecies of tigers, three of which are extinct: **Sumatran**, **Siberian**, **Indian** (or Bengal), **South China**, **Malayan**, **Indo-Chinese**, **Bali** (extinct), **Javan** (extinct) and **Caspian** (extinct).

•••

The largest subspecies of tiger is the Siberian tiger. An adult male can weigh up to 300 kg (660 lbs).

•••

The smallest subspecies of tiger is the Sumatran tiger. An adult male weighs between 100 to 140 kg (220 to 310 lb).

Tigers don't only have striped fur — their skin is striped too! They are the only truly striped cats.

•••

No two tigers have the same stripes, and their stripes are not symmetrical on both sides of their bodies.

•••

The stripes on a Sumatran tiger are closer together than on any of the other species.

•••

Tigers have tails that are about three feet long; they help them to stay balanced when taking tight corners.

A female Bengal tiger.

The oldest tiger on record was 26 years old.

•••

Tigers cause more human deaths through direct attack than any other mammal in the world.

•••

Tiger cubs stay with their mums for around two years before leaving their home range to start their own.

•••

Tigers aren't fully grown until the age of five.

•••

Tigers mostly hunt at night and alone. However, if an opportunity arises in the daytime to get a meal, they won't ignore it!

Tigers are fast! They can reach speeds of 49-65 km/h (30-40 m/ph).

•••

Only one in 2-20 tiger hunts end in a successful kill.

•••

When tigers hunt, they usually attack their prey's throat while holding them down.

•••

Tigers often take their kill to a safe place and bury it under vegetation to protect it from other predators that might steal it.

•••

Tigers can go for two weeks without eating. But when they do eat, they consume up to 34 kg (75 lb) of meat at one time!

A Sumatran tiger.

The **gestation period** (length of pregnancy) of a tiger is just under three months. They usually give birth to two or three cubs.

•••

When cubs are born, they are completely blind and helpless. Their mothers take care of them for two years, until they are strong enough to fend for themselves.

•••

Unlike most cats, tigers are very good swimmers. You can often see them crossing rivers and lakes. They also enjoy playing in water to stay cool on hot days.

Tigers don't live in prides like lions do. They mostly like to be on their own, but they do have home ranges that they stick to when roaming and hunting.

•••

When tigers do form groups, they are called '**streaks**'.

•••

Tigers have two types of roars: a 'true' roar and a 'coughing' roar. The true roar is longer, and the coughing roar is sharper and shorter, with their teeth exposed.

•••

You can hear a tiger's 'true' roar from up to 3 km (1.9 mi) away.

A Siberian tiger cub.

Tigers' hind legs are longer than their front legs. This gives them the amazing ability to leap up to 10m (33 ft).

•••

Tigers have padded feet, which help them stay silent while stalking their prey. The front pads of male tigers are usually larger than females, which helps other tigers know which gender they are when they spot tracks.

•••

Tigers aren't too fussy about what they eat, but their favourite meals include antelope, deer, wild boar and buffalo.

Tigers have white spots on the backs of their ears, which some scientists believe are used as fake 'eyes' to scare off predators that are behind them. Others believe they are used to help tiger cubs follow their mums in tall grass.

•••

White tigers do exist (see photo on the right), however, they are rare. They usually have beautiful blue eyes.

•••

Tigers have round pupils, unlike domestic cats, which have slitted pupils. This is because domestic cats are nocturnal, whereas tigers are crepuscular, meaning they are most active in the mornings and evenings.

A rare white tiger.

Tiger wee, which they use to mark their territory, smells like buttered popcorn.

•••

Female tigers are called **tigresses**.

•••

Tigers cannot purr. Instead, they squint or close their eyes to show they are happy.

•••

One swipe from a tiger's front paw is enough to break a bear's skull or back.

•••

Three species of tigers have gone extinct over the last 80 years. Tigers have been listed as an endangered species since 1986 and we need to protect them.

Tiger numbers are still dropping fast. The global wild tiger population was estimated to be between 3,062 and 3,948 mature individuals, down from around 100,000 at the start of the 20th century.

A Bengal tiger.

JAGUARS

This magnificent animal is not only the largest wild cat native to the Americas, but also the third-largest in the world. Due to their elusive nature, jaguars are challenging to spot in the wild.

It's common for people to mistake jaguars for leopards, but there are several key differences between the two. Let's explore these differences and learn more about the amazing jaguar.

ANIMAL PROFILE

Scientific name: Panthera oncra

Lifespan: 12-15 years in the wild; up to 23 years in captivity

Conservation status: Near threatened

Location: Central and South America, with occasional sightings in Arizona, New Mexico and Texas.

Jaguars can only be found in the wild in the Americas—between south-western USA down to northern Argentina and Paraguay.

•••

Jaguars feature regularly in the ancient mythology of the Mayans and Aztecs.

•••

The scientific name for the jaguar is Panthera onca.

•••

Out of all the big cats, jaguars are the third largest after lions and tigers.

•••

Jaguars prefer to live in dense rainforests, however, they will sometimes venture to other areas.

The jaguar may resemble the leopard, but they are slightly larger and they have less, but more dense, rosettes (spots) with one or several white dots in the middle.

•••

Jaguars enjoy water and swimming, just like tigers.

•••

Jaguars will often leap from a tree or into water to surprise and attack their prey. They are opportunistic hunters, meaning they will eat almost anything, big or small, that they can.

•••

Jaguars are carnivores, meaning they only eat meat.

A jaguar.

Jaguars are solitary creatures, living and hunting alone. They only meet with other jaguars to mate, or while raising cubs.

•••

Male jaguars are usually 10-20% larger than female jaguars. They also roam further for hunting.

•••

The size of jaguars varies greatly. While on average they weigh 56-96 kg (123-212 lb), the largest known males weigh as much as 158 kg (348 lb) while the females as little as 36 kg (79 lb).

•••

You wouldn't want to get in the way of a jaguar: its jaw is incredibly powerful, allowing it to break bones and tear open the hard shells of reptiles.

Argentina's national rugby team's emblem has a symbol of a jaguar on it. However, they are called Los Pumas (the pumas).

•••

The main threat to jaguars is deforestation. Many rainforests are being cut down, leaving the jaguars unable to survive.

•••

President Thomas Jefferson first recorded jaguars as an animal of the Americas in 1799.

•••

Few jaguars are still found in the USA, however, there are occasional sightings in New Mexico and Arizona. Many conservationists are fighting to protect them.

An American jaguar.

A black jaguar (also known as a black panther).

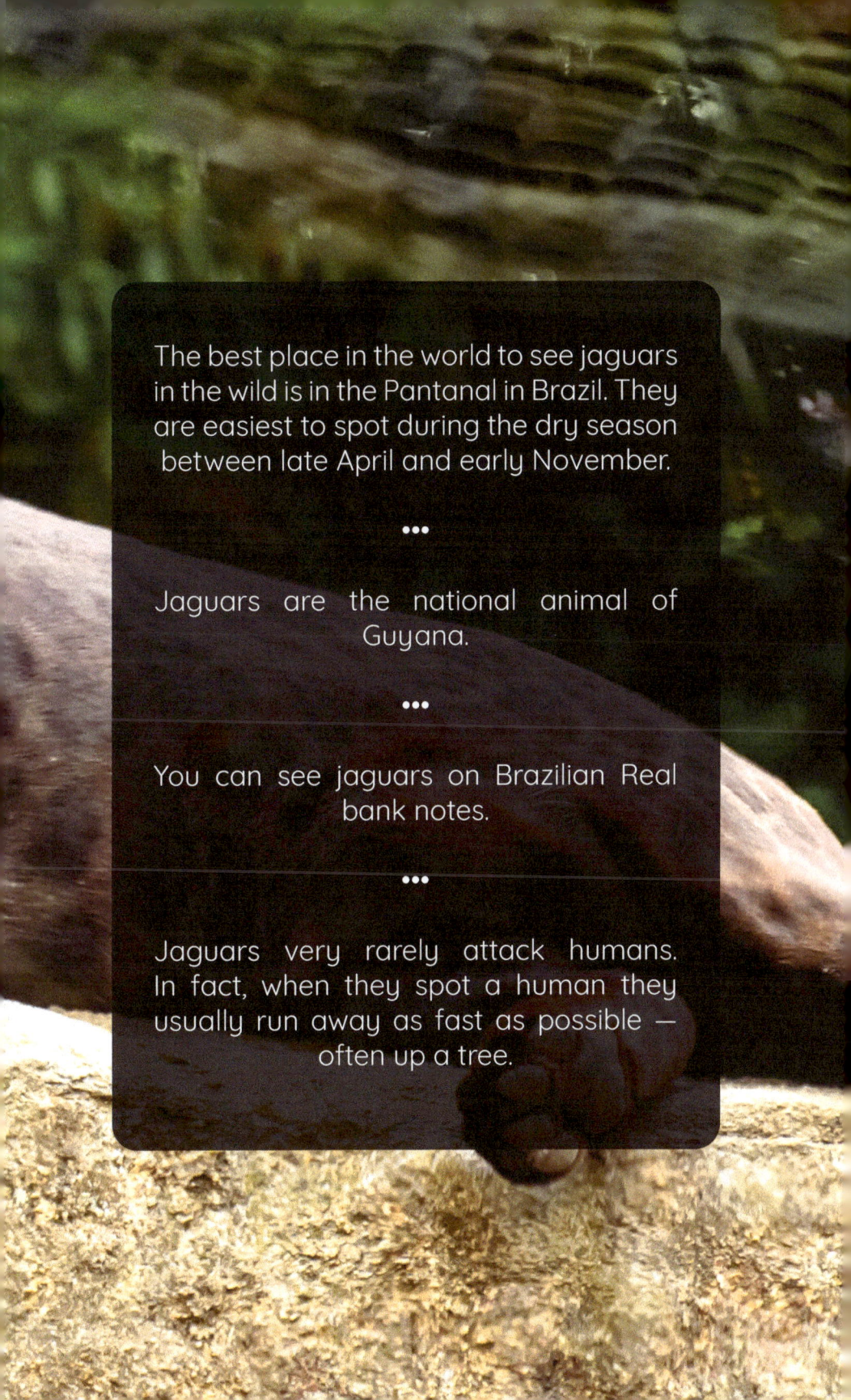

The best place in the world to see jaguars in the wild is in the Pantanal in Brazil. They are easiest to spot during the dry season between late April and early November.

•••

Jaguars are the national animal of Guyana.

•••

You can see jaguars on Brazilian Real bank notes.

•••

Jaguars very rarely attack humans. In fact, when they spot a human they usually run away as fast as possible — often up a tree.

Jaguars are some of the longest-living types of cat. In the wild, they live between 12-15 years, while in captivity they can live up to the age of 23.

•••

The word 'jaguar' is believed to have come from the word 'yaguara', meaning 'beast of prey' in the Tupian language (a group of 70 languages spoken in South America).

•••

Not all jaguars have spots. Around 6% of jaguars are black. Black jaguars are often referred to as black panthers. There are also very rare white, albino jaguars.

A female jaguar.

Jaguar cubs first join their mothers on hunts at the age of six months. They will learn from her for one to two years before setting off on their own.

Jaguars are classified as being 'Near Threatened', which means their population is decreasing.

•••

Jaguars define their territories by marking the boundaries with urine, feces and scratchings on trees.

•••

Sir David Attenborough called jaguars "the killers of killers", because of their unscrupulous attitude towards killing its prey.

•••

Jaguars used to exist in Eurasia, and according to fossil records they were 15-20% larger than the jaguars we know today.

LEOPARDS

The leopard, famous for its beautiful spots, is characterised by its shorter legs and large skull, when compared to other wild cats. It is also one of the world's most adaptable cats — able to survive and thrive in a wide range of habitats.

Here are some amazing facts about this spotted beauty.

Animal Profile

Scientific name: Panthera pardus

Lifespan: 12-17 years in the wild; up to 23 years in captivity

Conservation status: Near-threatened

Location: Sub-saharan and northeast Africa, central Asia, India and China.

The Persian leopard is the national animal of Iran (jointly with the Asiatic Lion).

•••

Leopards growl when angry and purr when happy, just like domestic cats.

•••

Leopards are mostly solitary cats, hunting and living alone. In Kruger National Park, researchers have found that most leopards stay at least 1 km (0.62 mi) apart from each other.

•••

Asian leopards, which are much smaller cats, hunt at different times of the day to tigers to avoid competition.

There are eight subspecies of leopard: **African leopard, Indian leopard, Javan leopard, Arabian leopard, Persian leopard, Amur leopard, Indochinese leopard** and the **Sri Lankan leopard**.

•••

Leopards are renowned for their agility. They can reach speeds of up to 58 km/h (36 mph).

•••

Leopards look similar to jaguars, except they have lighter frames and their rosettes (spots) are typically smaller and further apart.

•••

The earliest leopard fossils date back to over 600,000 years ago in in Europe. Paleontologists have also found leopard fossils in Japan.

Leopards have soft and thick fur, with even softer fur on their bellies.

•••

Out of all big cats, leopards have the largest distribution. You can find leopards living in Africa, Asia and the Caucasus. Leopards in far-eastern Russia live in areas where the winter temperatures can be as low as -25 °C (-13 °F).

•••

Although leopards are very adaptable to many environments, they usually prefer rocky areas with dense vegetation, so that they can hide.

•••

Leopards can be found in some urban areas of sub-saharan Africa.

Leopards have been crossbred with other big cat species to form hybrids. The most common hybrid is a lioness with a male leopard, producing **leopons**.

•••

Leopards have very good hearing and vision, which makes them great hunters. They can hear 5 times better than humans.

•••

Leopards mostly hunt at night, however, they have been seen hunting during the day in parts of western Africa.

•••

Leopards prefer to eat medium-sized prey, such as impala, bushbuck and chital. However, they occasionally hunt smaller carnivores such as cheetahs and foxes.

An African leopard in a tree.

Leopards are the smallest of the big cats. The average leopard is between 3 to 6.2 feet (92 to 190 centimeters) in length.

•••

The leopards' spots help to camouflage them, particularly when they are hiding in trees — which they love to do.

•••

Leopards often drag their prey into trees, to stop other animals from stealing it.

•••

Leopards usually give birth to a litter of two or three cubs. Leopard cubs don't leave their mother's den until they are three months old.

At 12-18 months old, leopard cubs are ready to live on their own.

• • •

Leopards aren't yet endangered, but their numbers are shrinking because their habitats are being destroyed. They are listed as a near-threatened species by the IUCN's Red List of Threatened Species.

• • •

Why are they called leopards? The name leopard is believed to have come from the Greek words leon (lion) and pardus (panther).

• • •

It might be confusing, but the genus of cats called Leopardus, does not include leopards! It does include cats such as ocelots, margays and pampas cats.

A close-up of a leopard.

What is the leopard's biggest and only predator? Humans! Sadly, humans hunt leopards for their beautiful fur and for Chinese medicine.

•••

The colour of a leopard's coat depends on where it lives. Warm-climate leopards have light yellow, tawny coloured coats, whereas those that live in dense forests have darker, reddish-orange coats.

•••

East African leopards have circular spots, whereas southern African leopards have square spots.

SNOW LEOPARDS

The snow leopard is the most elusive of the big cats, and is very rarely seen in the wild. Unlike other big cats, which mostly live in warmer climates, snow leopards thrive in harsh, cold environments.

Despite what many people think, the snow leopard is its own species, and although similar in many ways to the leopard, they are more closely related to tigers!

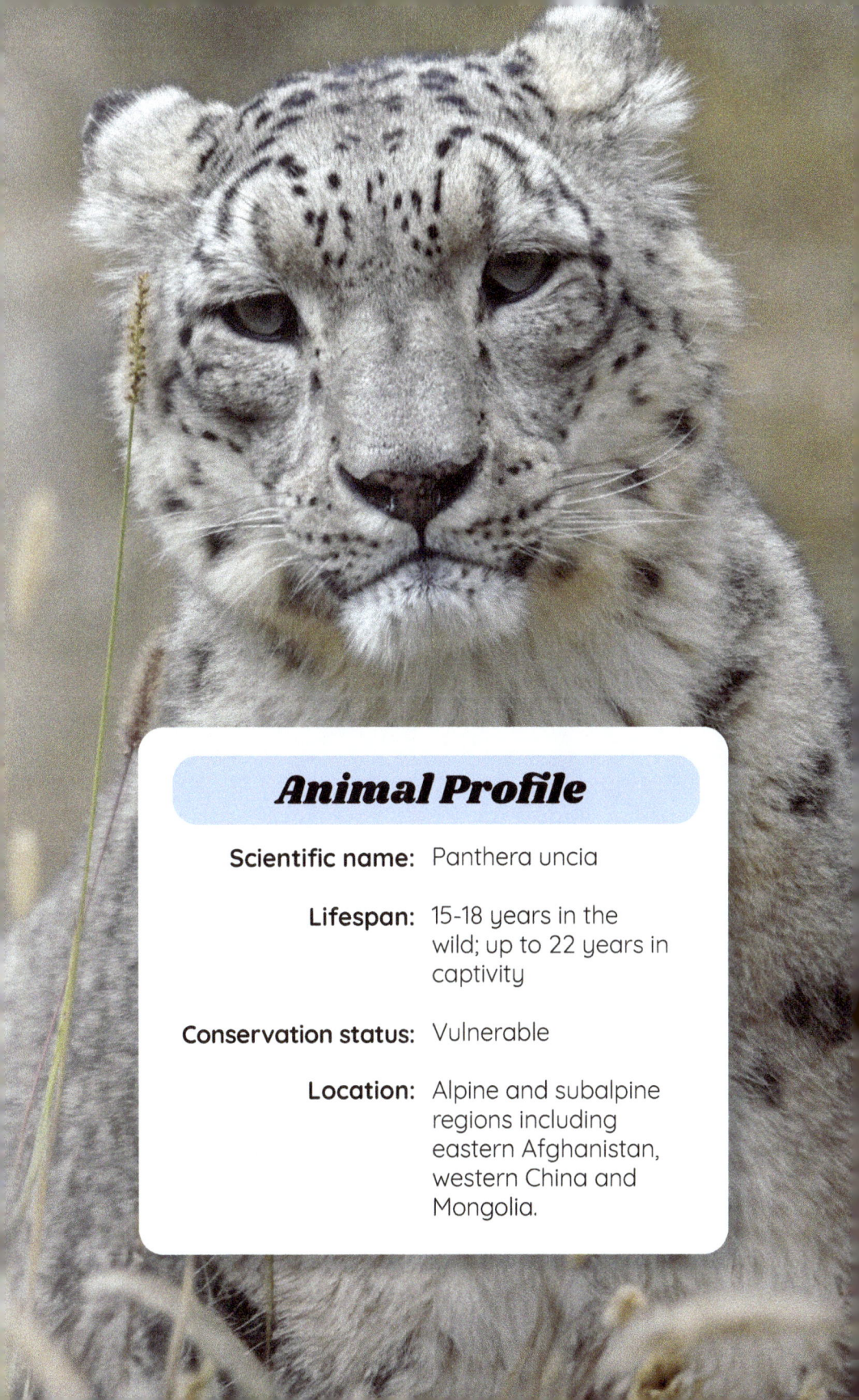

Animal Profile

Scientific name: Panthera uncia

Lifespan: 15-18 years in the wild; up to 22 years in captivity

Conservation status: Vulnerable

Location: Alpine and subalpine regions including eastern Afghanistan, western China and Mongolia.

Two young snow leopards.

Snow leopards are the only type of big cats that aren't able to roar.

•••

The snow leopard is the national animal of Afghanistan.

•••

Although their name suggests that they are closely related to leopards, snow leopards are actually genetically closer to tigers.

•••

The snow leopard's scientific name is Panthera uncia.

•••

Snow leopards have whitish fur with black spots on their head and neck, and larger rosettes on the rest of their backs, sides and tail. Their bellies are white and fluffy.

Snow leopards are the only big cats that live in the cold deserts of Asia.

•••

The snow leopard is also known as an 'ounce'.

•••

Snow leopards spend most of their time alone, which is why they are often referred to as 'the ghosts of the mountain'.

•••

You can find snow leopards across central and southern Asia.

•••

Look at a snow leopard's tail. It's very long! In fact, their tails are almost as long as their bodies.

Snow leopards aren't the largest of cats, but they can prey on animals that are three times their own weight.

•••

The fur on a snow leopard's belly is nearly 5 inches (12.7 cm) thick to keep them warm in cold, icy conditions.

•••

Although they can't roar, snow leopards make a range of other noises including growling, yowling and meowing.

•••

A study conducted by the WWF found that there were snow leopards living at 5,859 metres above sea level, which is around the same height as Canada's highest mountain.

Sadly, there are fewer than 10,000 snow leopards left in the wild, due to poachers and the loss of their habitats.

Because of their rapidly declining population, snow leopards are listed as Vulnerable on the IUCN Red List.

•••

Snow leopards are a monotypic species, which means there is just one variety of them, unlike other big cats that have several subspecies.

•••

Snow leopards can travel in snow that is up to 33 inches (85 cm) deep, although they often try to walk in the less-snowy path of other animals if they can.

•••

Most snow leopards weigh between 48.5-121 lbs (22-55 kg), although male snow leopards can weigh up to 165 lbs (75 kg).

Snow leopards have pale green or grey eyes.

•••

Snow leopards very rarely attack humans. In fact, there are only two known cases where this has happened.

•••

Female snow leopards give birth in rocky dens, which are lined with fur that has shed from their underbellies.

•••

Snow leopards actively hunt their prey, and have been known to prey on domestic livestock in more built-up areas.

Snow leopards like to attack from above. They often hide on a rocky outcrop, before ambushing their prey.

• • •

Although they are carnivores, snow leopards also eat large amounts of grass and twigs.

• • •

Snow leopards have small, rounded ears, which help to prevent heat loss.

Spot the difference!

Am I a leopard, jaguar, lion, tiger or snow leopard?!

1. _____

2. _____

3. _____

4. _____

5. _____

Big Cats Word Search

```
B V U L N E R A B L E Q
E S L I O N N H G J X D
D N N E K H F S Q A M N
P G D Q O E W S Z G B V
A F S A W P H G F U S B
N F D Z N V A X C A M I
T E R B Z G X R V R G G
H I N V C X E Q D S C
E Y G Y H D V R X E V A
R T U E I O P V E P L T
A R W E R C V B N D Z S
E S N O W L E O P A R D
```

Can you find all the words below in the word search puzzle on the left?

LION	JAGUAR	PANTHERA
TIGER	SNOW LEOPARD	BIG CATS
LEOPARD	VULNERABLE	ENDANGERED

SOLUTIONS

	V	U	L	N	E	R	A	B	L	E	
E		L	I	O	N				J		
	N		E						A		
P		D		O					G		
A			A		P				U		B
N				N		A			A		I
T					G		R		R		G
H		I				E		D			C
E		G					R				A
R			E					E			T
A				R					D		S
	S	N	O	W	L	E	O	P	A	R	D

SPOT THE DIFFERENCE

1. Leopard

2. Tiger

3. Lion

4. Jaguar

5. Snow leopard

AND THAT'S ALL, FOLKS!

As we reach the end of this fur-tastic journey, we hope you enjoyed every moment!

Your feedback means the world to us, and we kindly ask you to share your thoughts with a **review on whichever platform you purchased this book**.

Not only do your words bring us joy, but they also guide fellow readers in choosing the perfect book for their young adventurers.

Thank you again for your support!

For more great books and giveaways, visit us at:

www.bellanovabooks.com

ALSO BY JENNY KELLETT

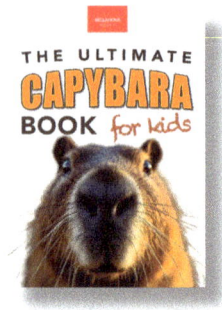  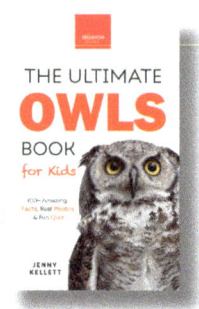

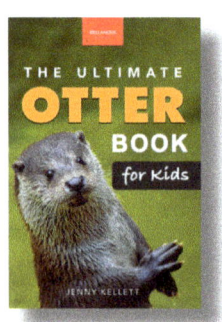 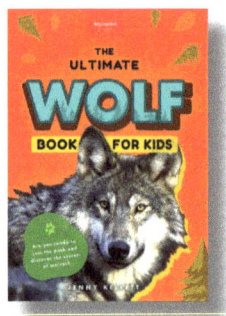 

... and more!

Available at

www.bellanovabooks.com

and all major online bookstores.

SOURCES

Tigers

- Staff, L. (2010). Iconic Cats: All 9 Subspecies of Tigers. Retrieved 2 March 2020, from https://www.livescience.com/29822-tiger-subspecies-images.html
- Siberian tiger. (2020). Retrieved 2 March 2022, from https://en.wikipedia.org/wiki/Siberian_tiger
- Sumatran tiger. (2020). Retrieved 2 March 2022, from https://en.wikipedia.org/wiki/Sumatran_tiger
- Facts, T. (2020). Tiger Facts. Retrieved 2 March 2022, from https://www.nationalgeographic.com.au/animals/tiger-facts.aspx
- All About Tigers - Physical Characteristics | SeaWorld Parks & Entertainment. (2020). Retrieved 2 March 2022, from https://seaworld.org/animals/all-about/tiger/characteristics/
- Sunquist, M. (2010). "What is a Tiger? Ecology and Behaviour". In R. Tilson; P. J. Nyhus (eds.). Tigers of the World: The Science, Politics and Conservation of Panthera tigris (Second ed.). London, Burlington: Academic Press. p. 19–34. ISBN 978-0-08-094751-8.
- Novak, R. M.; Walker, E. P. (1999). "Panthera tigris (tiger)". Walker's Mammals of the World (6th ed.). Baltimore: Johns Hopkins University Press. pp. 825–828. ISBN 978-0-8018-5789-8.
- "Sympatric Tiger and Leopard: How two big cats coexist in the same area". Archived from the original on 13 February 2020. Ecology.info
- Sankhala, K. S. (1967). "Breeding behaviour of the tiger Panthera tigris in Rajasthan". International Zoo Yearbook. 7 (1): 133–147. doi:10.1111/j.1748-1090.1967.tb00354.x.

- Sunquist, M.; Sunquist, F. (1991). "Tigers". In Seidensticker, J.; Lumpkin, S. (eds.). Great Cats. Fog City Press. pp. 97–98. ISBN 978-1-875137-90-9.
- McDougal, Charles (1977). The Face of the Tiger. London: Rivington Books and André Deutsch. pp. 63–76.
- Mazák, V. (1981). "Panthera tigris" (PDF). Mammalian Species. 152(152): 1–8. doi:10.2307/3504004. JSTOR 3504004. Archived from the original (PDF)on 9 March 2020.
- Matthiessen, P.; Hornocker, M. (2008). Tigers In The Snow (reprint ed.). Paw Prints. ISBN 9781435296152.
- Hayward, M. W.; Jędrzejewski, W.; Jędrzejewska, B. (2012). "Prey preferences of the tiger Panthera tigris". Journal of Zoology. 286 (3): 221–231. doi:10.1111/j.1469-7998.2011.00871.x.
- Leyhausen, P. (1979). Cat behavior: the predatory and social behavior of domestic and wild cats. Berlin: Garland Publishing, Incorporated. p. 281. ISBN 9780824070175.
- Robinson, R. (1969). "The white tigers of Rewa and gene homology in the Felidae". Genetica. 40 (1): 198−200. doi:10.1007/BF01787350.
- Brooke, C., & Brooke, C. (2013). 10 of the Most Interesting (and Unusual) Tiger Facts | Featured Creature. Retrieved 3 March 2020, from https://featuredcreature.com/10-of-the-most-interesting-and-unusual-tiger-facts/

Jaguars

- Seymour, K. L. (1989). "Panthera onca" (PDF). Mammalian Species. 340 (340): 1–9. doi:10.2307/3504096. JSTOR 3504096. Archived from the original (PDF) on 20 June 2010.
- All about Jaguars: Ecology". Wildlife Conservation Society. Archived from the original on 29 May 2009.
- Jaguar. (2020). Retrieved 3 March 2020, from https://en.wikipedia.org/wiki/Jaguar#cite_note-WCS-23

- Nowell, K.; Jackson, P., eds. (1996). "Panthera Onca" (PDF). Wild Cats. Status Survey and Conservation Action Plan. Gland, Switzerland: IUCN/SSC Cat Specialist Group. IUCN. pp. 118–122.
- Baker, Natural History and Behavior, pp. 8–16.
- Nowak, Ronald M (1999). Walker's Mammals of the World. 2. Baltimore: Johns Hopkins University Press. p. 831. ISBN 978-0-8018-5789-8.
- Burnien, David; Wilson, Don E. (2001). Animal: The Definitive Visual Guide to the World's Wildlife. New York City: Dorling Kindersley. ISBN 978-0-7894-7764-4.
- Boitani, Luigi (1984). Simon and Schuster's Guide to Mammals. Simon & Schuster. ISBN 978-0-671-43727-5.
- Davies, Sean (26 July 2007). "Puma power: Argentinian rugby". bbc.co.uk. Retrieved 8 October 2007.
- Quigley, H.; Foster, R.; Petracca, L.; Payan, E.; Salom, R.; Harmsen, B. (2017). "Panthera onca". IUCN Red List of Threatened Species. IUCN. 2017: e.T15953A123791436. doi:10.2305/IUCN.UK.2017-3.RLTS.T15953A50658693.en
- North American jaguar
- "Jaguar Fact Sheet". Jaguar Species Survival Plan. American Zoo and Aquarium Association. Archived from the original on 27 January 2012.
- Jaguar Fact Sheet". Jaguar Species Survival Plan. American Zoo and Aquarium Association. Archived from the original on 27 January 2012. Retrieved 14 August 2022.
- Dinets, V.; Polechla, P. J. (2005). "First documentation of melanism in the jaguar (Panthera onca) from northern Mexico". Cat News. 42: 18. Archived from the original on 26 September 2020.
- Jeff Egerton (Spring 2006). "Jaguars: Magnificence in the Southwest" (PDF). Newsletter. Archived from the original (PDF) on 21 July 2011.
- 10 Roaring Facts About Jaguars. (2017). Retrieved 3 March 2020, from https://www.mentalfloss.com/article/91382/10-roaring-facts-about-jaguars
- Panthera onca :: Florida Museum of Natural History. (2020).

Retrieved 3 March 2020, from https://www.floridamuseum.ufl.edu/florida-vertebrate-fossils/species/panthera-onca/

Lions

- Smuts, G. L.; Robinson, G. A.; Whyte, I. J. (1980). "Comparative growth of wild male and female lions (Panthera leo)". Journal of Zoology. 190 (3): 365–373. Bibcode:2010JZoo..281..263G. doi:10.1111/j.1469-7998.1980.tb01433.x.
- Chellam, R. and A. J. T. Johnsingh (1993). "Management of Asiatic lions in the Gir Forest, India". In Dunstone, N.; Gorman, M. L. (eds.). Mammals as predators: the proceedings of a symposium held by the Zoological Society of London and the Mammal Society, London. Volume 65 of Symposia of the Zoological Society of London. London: Zoological Society of London. pp. 409–23.
- Biggest Lion ever Recorded . (2020). Retrieved 28 February 2020, from https://www.ligerworld.com/biggest-lion-ever-recorded.html
- How Fast Can a Lion Run? Learn the Full Story. (2019). Retrieved 28 February 2020, from https://africafreak.com/how-fast-can-a-lion-run
- Eklund, R.; Peters, G.; Ananthakrishnan, G.; Mabiza, E. (2011). "An acoustic analysis of lion roars. I: Data collection and spectrogram and waveform analyses"(PDF). Speech, Music and Hearing Quarterly Progress and Status Report. 51: 1.
- Bauer, H.; Van Der Merwe, S. (2002). "The African lion database". Cat News. 36: 41–53.
- Chardonnet, P. (2002). Conservation of African lion (PDF). Paris, France: International Foundation for the Conservation of Wildlife. Archived from the original (PDF) on 10 November 2013.
- Schaller, pp. 120–21.
- Trivedi, B. P. (2002). "Female Lions Prefer Dark-Maned

- Males, Study Finds". National Geographic News. National Geographic. Retrieved 1 September 2007.
- Koenigswald, W. v. (2002). Lebendige Eiszeit: Klima und Tierwelt im Wandel (in German). Stuttgart: Theiss. ISBN 978-3-8062-1734-6.
- Koenigswald, W. v. (2002). Lebendige Eiszeit: Klima und Tierwelt im Wandel (in German). Stuttgart: Theiss. ISBN 978-3-8062-1734-6.
- Lions in Captivity - Feline Facts and Information. (2020). Retrieved 28 February 2020, from https://www.felineworlds.com/lions-in-captivity/
- Ligers and Tigons, Oh My! Cat Lineage Littered with Interbreeding". Livescience.com. 2016-01-15. Retrieved 2016-04-06.
- Turner, J. A.; Vasicek, C. A.; Somers, M. J. (2015). "Effects of a colour variant on hunting ability: the white lion in South Africa". Open Science Repository Biology: e45011830.
- What Makes Lionesses Better Hunters Than Lions?. (2020). Retrieved 28 February 2020, from https://www.forbes.com/sites/quora/2018/05/16/what-makes-lionesses-better-hunters-than-lions/#6159b90f4a6f
- Schaller, p. 153.
- Hemmer, H. (2011). "The story of the cave lion - Panthera Leo Spelaea (Goldfuss, 1810) - A review". Quaternaire. 4: 201–208.
- Menon, V. (2003). A Field Guide to Indian Mammals. New Delhi: Dorling Kindersley India. ISBN 978-0-14-302998-4.
- Schoe, M.; Sogbohossou, E. A.; Kaandorp, J.; De Iongh, H. (2010). Progress Report – collaring operation Pendjari Lion Project, Benin. The Dutch Zoo Conservation Fund (for funding the project).
- Brakefield, T. (1993). "Lion: Sociable Simba". Big Cats: Kingdom of Might. London: Voyageur Press. pp. 50–67. ISBN 978-0-89658-329-0.
- A Whole New World of Simba: 10 Amazing Facts About These Big Cats for World Lion Day. (2016). Retrieved 28 February 2020, from https://www.natureworldnews.com/articles/26630/20160811/world-lion-day.htm
- Ford, Paul (2005). Companion to Narnia: Revised Edition. San

Francisco: HarperCollins. p. 6. ISBN 978-0-06-079127-8.
- Animal Planet. (2020). From the Field. [online] Available at: http://www.animalplanet.com/tv-shows/wild-kingdom/about-animals/lions-field/ [Accessed 28 Feb. 2020].
- Amount of Food a Lion Eats. (2020). Retrieved 28 February 2020, from https://animals.mom.me/amount-food-lion-eats-9881.html
- Lions Of Africa- Physical Characteristics. (2020). Retrieved 1 March 2020, from http://www.chakarov.com/studentswork/lions
- Main, D. (2013). Becoming King: Why So Few Male Lions Survive to Adulthood . Retrieved 1 March 2020, from https://www.livescience.com/41572-male-lion-survival.html
- Daniel Peel V. (2011). Lion Anatomy- The Eye. Retrieved 1 March 2020, from https://danielpeel.wordpress.com/2011/10/03/lion-anatomy-the-eye/
- Africa: Tanzania Has Largest Number of Lions in Africa, New Report Says. (2019). Retrieved 1 March 2020, from https://allafrica.com/stories/201908120146.html
- Lion Reproduction & Offspring of the African Lion | ALERT. (2020). Retrieved 1 March 2020, from https://lionalert.org/lion-reproduction-offspring/
- Lion Pictures. (2020). Retrieved 2 March 2020, from https://www.thoughtco.com/lion-pictures-4122962
- Contributor, A. (2019). Lions: Facts & Information. Retrieved 2 March 2020, from https://www.livescience.com/27404-lion-facts.html
- Lion. (2020). Retrieved 2 March 2020, from https://en.wikipedia.org/wiki/Lion

Leopards

- A-Z, A., 10s, A., Endangered, M., Jumpers, H., Living, L., & Change, E. et al. (2020). Amazing Facts about Leopards | OneKindPlanet Animal Education & Facts. Retrieved 3 March 2020, from https://onekindplanet.org/animal/leopard/
- Izawa, M.; Nakanishi, N. (2015). "Felidae". In Ohdachi, S. D.; Ishi-

- bashi, Y.; Iwasa, M. A.; Saitoh, T. (eds.). The Wild Mammals of Japan (Second ed.). Kyoto: Shoukadoh Book Sellers and the Mammalogical Society of Japan. pp. 226−231. ISBN 978-4-87974-691-7.
- Ghezzo, E.; Rook, L. (2015). "The remarkablePanthera pardus (Felidae, Mammalia) record from Equi (Massa, Italy): taphonomy, morphology, and paleoecology". Quaternary Science Reviews. 110 (110): 131–151. doi:10.1016/j.quascirev.2014.12.020.
- Mills, M. G. L. (2005). "Subfamily Pantherinae". In Skinner, J. D.; Chimimba, C. T. (eds.). The mammals of the southern African subregion (Third ed.). Cambridge: Cambridge University Press. pp. 385–396. ISBN 9780521844185.
- Uphyrkina, O.; Johnson, E. W.; Quigley, H.; Miquelle, D.; Marker, L.; Bush, M.; O'Brien, S. J. (2001). "Phylogenetics, genome diversity and origin of modern leopard, Panthera pardus" (PDF). Molecular Ecology. 10(11): 2617–2633. doi:10.1046/j.0962-1083.2001.01350.x. PMID 11883877.
- Kisling, V.N., ed. (2001). Zoo and Aquarium History : Ancient Animal Collections to Zoological Gardens. Boca Raton, Florida (USA): CRC Press. p. 314. ISBN 978-0-8493-2100-9.
- Mills, M. G. L.; Hes, L. (1997). The Complete Book of Southern African Mammals. Cape Town, South Africa: Struik Publishers. pp. 178–180. ISBN 978-0-947430-55-9.
- Hayward, M.W.; Henschel, P.; O'Brien, J.; Hofmeyr, M.; Balme, G.; Kerley, G. I. H. (2006). "Prey preferences of the leopard (Panthera pardus)" (PDF). Journal of Zoology. 270 (4): 298–313. Bibcode:2010JZoo..281..263G. doi:10.1111/j.1469-7998.2006.00139.x.
- Leopard | San Diego Zoo Animals & Plants. (2020). Retrieved 26 March 2020, from https://animals.sandiegozoo.org/animals/leopard
- Leopard | National Geographic. (2020). Retrieved 26 March 2020, from https://www.nationalgeographic.com/animals/mammals/l/leopard/
- Contributor, A. (2014). Facts About Leopards. Retrieved 26

- March 2020, from https://www.livescience.com/27403-leopards.html
- Program)), U., Program), D., (Panthera), P., (Panthera), G., (WCS), V., & SG), A. et al. (2015). IUCN Red List of Threatened Species: Leopard. IUCN Red List Of Threatened Species. Retrieved from https://www.iucnredlist.org/species/15954/163991139
- They have the largest range of all the big cats but humans are putting their habitats in jeopardy. (2013). Retrieved 26 March 2020, from https://www.awf.org/wildlife-conservation/leopard
- Kitchener, A. C.; Breitenmoser-Würsten, C.; Eizirik, E.; Gentry, A.; Werdelin, L.; Wilting, A.; Yamaguchi, N.; Abramov, A. V.; Christiansen, P.; Driscoll, C.; Duckworth, J. W.; Johnson, W.; Luo, S.-J.; Meijaard, E.; O'Donoghue, P.; Sanderson, J.; Seymour, K.; Bruford, M.; Groves, C.; Hoffmann, M.; Nowell, K.; Timmons, Z.; Tobe, S. (2017). "A revised taxonomy of the Felidae: The final report of the Cat Classification Task Force of the IUCN Cat Specialist Group" (PDF). Cat News (Special Issue 11): 73–75.

Snow Leopards

- 7 fascinating facts about snow leopards. (2018). Retrieved 30 March 2020, from https://blog.wwf.ca/blog/2018/09/24/7-fascinating-facts-about-snow-leopards/
- McCarthy, T.; Mallon, D.; Jackson, R.; Zahler, P. & McCarthy, K. (2017). "Panthera uncia". IUCN Red List of Threatened Species. IUCN. 2017: e.T22732A50664030.
- McCarthy, T. M. & Chapron, G., eds. (2003). Snow Leopard Survival Strategy (PDF). Seattle, USA: International Snow Leopard Trust and Snow Leopard Network.
- Sunquist, M.; Sunquist, F. (2002). "Snow leopard Uncia

- uncia (Schreber, 1775)". Wild Cats of the World. Chicago: University of Chicago Press. pp. 377–394. ISBN 978-0-226-77999-7.
- Facts, A. (2020). Snow leopard guide: habitat, diet and conservation. Retrieved 30 March 2020, from https://www.discoverwildlife.com/animal-facts/mammals/facts-about-snow-leopards/
- Chadwick, D. H. (2008). "Out of the Shadows". National Geographic. Retrieved 2020-01-29.
- McCarthy, T. M. & Chapron, G., eds. (2003). Snow Leopard Survival Strategy (PDF). Seattle, USA: International Snow Leopard Trust and Snow Leopard Network.

www.ingramcontent.com/pod-product-compliance
Lightning Source LLC
LaVergne TN
LVHW050132080526
838202LV00061B/6474